| | DATE DUE | | |
|---|---|---|---|
| V 29 01 | | | |
| | | | |
| | | | |
| | | | |
| | | | |
| | | | |
| | | | |
| | | | |
| | | | |
| | | | |
| | | | |

# BOOK *of* HOURS

*Illuminations by Simon Marmion*

WITH AN INTRODUCTION AND COMMENTARY

*by James Thorpe*

THE HUNTINGTON LIBRARY · SAN MARINO, CALIFORNIA

This publication reproduces in color facsimile seventeen decorated leaves from the Huntington manuscript HM 1173, a Book of Hours made about 1450-1475. The vellum leaves are about 5 1/2" (14 cm) wide and 8 1/2" (21 cm) tall; the decorated portion of each leaf is about 4 3/4" by 7 1/4". The reproductions are same size as the originals.

Copyright © 1976
Henry E. Huntington Library and Art Gallery
1151 Oxford Road, San Marino, CA 91108

New edition, 1990

ISBN: 0-87328-130-6

Library of Congress Catalog Card Number: 90-4663
Printed in the United States of America by PSP Graphics, Canoga Park, California. Photography by Robert Schlosser, Huntington Library.

# *Contents*

# *Acknowledgment*

Jean Preston, former Curator of Manuscripts of the Huntington Library, gave valuable assistance in the preparation of the reproductions and of the introductory material for the original 1976 edition of *Book of Hours.* The revised 1990 edition was produced under the guidance of Mary L. Robertson, Curator of Manuscripts of the Huntington Library.

# Introduction

T HIS LITTLE BOOK offers a rich feast for the eyes. It presents, in color facsimile, the seventeen miniature paintings in a magnificent fifteenth-century Book of Hours in the notable collection of the Huntington Library.

These paintings are generally attributed to Simon Marmion, a master of the art of the miniature, one of the highest forms of artistic achievement of the Middle Ages. They are of outstanding beauty, and even reproductions of them can convey some sense of their rich appeal. This introduction and the short commentary on the page facing each plate are intended to help bridge the five centuries which separate these paintings from us. The reward is, ideally, to be able to look at the pictures with a freshened understanding.

In the late Middle Ages, rich people sometimes commissioned the preparation of a handwritten book to be used in private devotions. Such a book included psalms, other passages from the Bible, anthems, hymns, and prayers, and it usually had colorful decorations and pictures to give visual beauty. These devotional manuals were for laymen, and they came to be called Books of Hours because they generally included, as a central section, the material to be read in observing the "Hours" of the Virgin Mary.

In honoring the Virgin Mary, the twenty-four-hour day was divided (theoretically at least) into eight equal parts; each portion was called an "Hour," using the beginning of the period as its indicator. A short private service (called an "office") was set for the observance of that "Hour," and many of the "Offices" were given the name of the hour in the classical Roman counting. (Prime, for example, was the Roman first hour, or 6 a.m.; Terce the third hour, 9 a.m.; Sext the sixth hour, noon; and Nones the ninth hour, 3 p.m.)

A certain episode in the life of the Virgin Mary came to be associated with each "Hour," which was introduced by a picture portraying that episode. The conventional associations in one popular use were (to simplify somewhat) as follows:

| "Hour" | Office | Episode |
|---|---|---|
| 1. midnight | Matins (or Nocturns) | The Annunciation |
| 2. 3 a.m. | Lauds | The Visitation of Elizabeth |
| 3. 6 a.m. | Prime | The Nativity |
| 4. 9 a.m. | Terce | The Annunciation to the Shepherds |
| 5. noon | Sixt | The Adoration of the Magi |
| 6. 3 p.m. | Nones | The Presentation in the Temple |
| 7. 6 p.m. | Vespers | The Flight into Egypt |
| 8. 9 p.m | Compline | The Coronation of the Virgin |

Books of Hours include various other sections. Since they were usually made to order, the contents and the arrangements are not fixed. Usually they begin with a Calendar of Saints' Days, and continue with lessons from each of the four Gospels. Then the central part, the Hours of the Virgin Mary. The concluding part often has the Penitential Psalms and Litany, the Office of the Dead, and memorials to various saints.

Doubtless some people used their Books of Hours assiduously as an aid to salvation. But there were other uses as well. Books of Hours were—and are—a delight to the eye and the hand. The material used was vellum, calfskin or sheepskin which had been soaked in a caustic lime solution, scraped and shaved to an even thinness, rubbed smooth with pumice, stretched till dry, and then cut to size. A Book of Hours was prepared by a group of professionals, often in a single workshop under a master. First the text—lettered in uniform calligraphy—was written with a quill pen by a scribe. Then the ornamental borders of styled sprays and branches, of leaves and of flowers, were drawn by a specialist, using red and other colors. The pictures were then painted by another artist, usually the master, and they were sometimes major works of art within the small size of a miniature.

There was often a sense of magnificence about the whole Book of Hours, aided by the rare materials used, such as gold for notable decoration, lapis lazuli from Persia for making ultramarine, indigo from Bengal, and gums from Arabia. The lavish use of gold was especially eye catching: it was applied in shining leaf form to the frames of the miniatures and to the decorated initial letters, and in paint form to the acanthus leaves in the borders and to heighten objects within the miniatures themselves. A Book of Hours was expensive, an esteemed gift on such a great occasion as a noble marriage, and highly valued by its owner; it could be looked at with pleasure and shown with delight. Today they are often still called by the name of the first owner.

The text was normally written in Latin, which was the common language of the Roman Catholic Church and the universal language among learned men in western Europe. Although many owners of Books of Hours could not read Latin (or much of any language), they knew most of the prayers by heart and used the pictures to find their place. A great center of interest was for them (as it is for most of us) the charm of the decorations and the meaningful beauty of the paintings.

The earliest Books of Hours date from the latter part of the thirteenth century, but their great flowering—both in quality and in quantity—was in the fifteenth century, particularly in France and Flanders. This brief but intense period of activity produced some major works of art. The spread of printing late in the fifteenth century foreshadowed their decline, and no more Books of Hours were done by hand after the early sixteenth century. For a short time, they were printed, with illustrations by woodcut or by hand; but the production of Books of Hours essentially ended with the Reformation of the sixteenth century.

The Book of Hours from which the plates in this publication are reproduced was made, it is thought, between about 1450 and 1475. Usually, the artists of Books of Hours are not identified, but this book has for many decades been attributed to Simon Marmion, on stylistic grounds. Marmion was a Franco-Flemish artist who was born in Amiens, between 1420 and 1425; he was the master of a workshop in Valenciennes, where he died in 1489. He was primarily an "illuminator" of manuscripts, though he was also a panel painter; he was called "Prince of Illuminators" by one contemporary poet, and he was also known as the "Master of Colors." I hope that these reproductions will indicate why he was given these names.

This Book of Hours is made up of 124 decorated vellum leaves. Each of its seventeen miniature paintings introduces a section, and the arrangement is a standard one. Plates 1-4 begin the Gospel lessons with paintings of the four Evangelists, St. John, St. Luke, St. Matthew, and St. Mark. Plates 5 and 6 introduce the Mass of the Virgin Mary and the Hours of the Cross. Plates 7-14 introduce the eight Offices in the Hours of the Virgin Mary, in the general order described above, which are the central part from which the term Book of Hours derives. Plates 15-17 begin the Penitential Psalms, the Prayers to the Virgin, and the Office of the Dead. Each plate is described in the explanatory note on the page facing it.

But the main reward that this little book offers is the chance to look at a series of miniature paintings of merit. People have different ways of looking at pictures, and there is ample opportunity here to perceive, by close observation, many of the effects, large and small, which are conveyed in the miniature scale of these pictures. The amount of convincing detail is remarkable. The Three Kings are portrayed individually, as are the soldiers at the Crucifixion, the shepherds in the field by night, and the crowd in the Temple. Most of the pictures tell a story, and the action is deftly revealed by posture as well as by expression. The background in many of them shows a wandering stream and the towers of a distant city; there are numerous trees, plants, birds, boats, and clouds; there are thatched roofs, tile floors, and a great variety of robes, cloaks, dresses, hats, and hair styles, all carefully distinguished. Most of these details of dress and landscape and buildings bear a realistic resemblance to fifteenth-century Flemish models. The rising perspective of the outdoor scenes almost lifts the viewer up to take part in the action. There is appeal in the range of colors, from the strong cerulean blue to the rich gold to the shadings of middle and light greens. A sense of delicacy and reality pervades these pictures, which are in actuality mainly symbolic scenes, the meanings of which reinforce—and are reinforced by—the Offices which they introduce.

The volume represented by these plates is one of a collection of some sixty-eight manuscript Books of Hours, on vellum, in the Huntington Library. Like all of the material in this Library, they have been collected for use by scholars in furthering their researches. Many of the chief treasures of the Library are always on exhibition for viewing by anyone who cares to visit. It is a pleasure to offer permanent possession, in a form close to the original, of the paintings from one splendid Book of Hours.

## Plate 1.  St. John on the Isle of Patmos

Plates 1-4 introduce the four Gospel lessons. Each plate portrays the Evangelist to whom the Gospel is attributed and includes the creature which was his symbol.

*Introducing the Lesson from the Gospel according to St. John: the beginning of the fourth Gospel, "In principio erat verbum" (In the beginning was the Word).*

St. John is seated on the rocky isle of Patmos (where, by tradition, he was exiled for a time and received a revelation), with rays of illumination descending toward him from above. An eagle, his symbol, is perched on a rock in front of him; the landscape behind him is richly decorated with a flourishing city, water, a boat, trees, and birds.

Inicium sci euuange
lii Sedm Iohannem.
IN principio erat uer
bum. et verbum erat

## Plate 2.  St. Luke Painting the Virgin Mary

*Introducing the Lesson from the Gospel according to St. Luke: the story of the Annunciation, from Luke, beginning "In illo tempore missus est angelus Gabriel" (At that time the angel Gabriel was sent).*

St. Luke, seated on a bench in front of an easel is painting a portrait of Mary and the infant Jesus, who appear in the arched opening behind a hanging brocade, with a trace of the outdoors visible behind her. An ox, St. Luke's symbol, lies on the tile floor in the left foreground. According to a tradition from the sixth century, Luke was (in addition to being a physician) an artist who painted many likenesses of Mary; doubtless this tradition arose from the vivid portrayal of the role of Mary in the Gospel according to St. Luke.

## Plate 3.  St. Matthew

*Introducing the Lesson from the Gospel according to St. Matthew: the story of the visit of the three Wise Men (Magi), from Matthew, beginning "Cum natus esset dominus Jesus in bethleem" (Now when Jesus was born in Bethlehem).*

St. Matthew is seated on a bench, writing in a book on a sloping desk. An angel, the figure which symbolizes St. Matthew, stands behind him holding a banner inscribed with the Latin form of his name.

Sequencia sancti euua
geln sedm matheum ;·
Um natus esset dūs
ihs in bethleem iude:

## Plate 4. St. Mark

*Introducing the Lesson from the Gospel according to St. Mark: the account of Jesus commissioning his disciples, the conclusion of the Gospel according to St. Mark, beginning "In illo tempore recambentibus undecim disciplis" (Afterward he appeared unto the eleven disciples).*

St. Mark is seated in a narrow room behind a sloping desk, writing on a scroll. A lion, his symbol, lies at his feet, and a distant landscape is visible through an open archway.

Sequentia sancti euua
gelii secundum marchum ҂
Nillo tempore: Recum
bentibus undecim disciplis

## Plate 5.  Virgin Enthroned between Angels

*Introducing the Mass of the Virgin Mary: the Office begins with a prayer,*
*"Salue sancta parens enixa puerpera regem" (Hail, holy parent, mother of the*
*King [of Heaven and Earth]).*

The Virgin Mary, holding the tiny Jesus, is seated on a Gothic throne
with elaborate open tracery, through which a landscape and distant
city can be seen. An angel kneels on the tile floor on each side, the
one on the left playing a lute and the one on the right playing a harp.

Et hy apres senseut la
messe de nostredame
Alue sancta parens enixa
puerpera regem q̃ celum

## Plate 6.  The Crucifixion

*Introducing the Office of the Hours of the Cross: the short version commences with the words "Domine labia mea aperies et os meum" (O Lord, open thou my lips. And my mouth [shall show forth thy praise]).*

The two kneeling figures on the left are Mary and (behind her) John, the disciple whom Jesus loved; behind them are two holy women. On the right is a group of four soldiers and burghers, in the distance are the towers of Jerusalem, and the bones in the foreground signify the name of the place where the crucifixion took place, Golgotha, or the place of a skull.

Chy sensieuuent lez
heures de la crois;
Omne labia mea
aprics Et os meu

## Plates 7-14. The Hours of the Virgin

These eight plates introduce the eight "Hours" (or Offices) in the twenty-four hour-day. This section of the manuscript is the literal "Book of Hours" and the basis for giving that title to the entire volume.

## Plate 7. The Annunciation

*Introducing the Office of Matins (midnight), the first of the Hours of the Virgin: it commences with the words "Domine labia mea aperies et os meum" (O Lord, open thou my lips. And my mouth [shall show forth thy praise]).*

The angel Gabriel appears (on the left) half kneeling to Mary (on the right) reading, to announce to her that she has found favor with God and will be the mother of Jesus. Out of his mouth come in tiny letters the words "Ave gracia plena" (Hail, thou that art highly favored, [the Lord is with thee: blessed art thou among women]). The dove, symbol of the Holy Spirit, comes down on golden rays to abide with Mary, who is raising her hands in surprise at the Annunciation (announcement).

Chy apres sensiewt
les heures de nredie
Dmine labia mea
aperies Et os meum

## Plate 8.  The Visitation

*Introducing the Office of Lauds (3 a.m.), the second of the Hours of the Virgin:*
*it commences with the words "Deus in adiutorium meum intende"*
*(O God, come to my help).*

When Mary was pregnant with Jesus, she went into the hill country
to tell her cousin Elizabeth, whose baby (to be John the Baptist)
leaped in the womb at Mary's greeting. Mary's response took the
form of the  anthem known as the Magnificat (My soul doth
magnify the Lord). Elizabeth( the older woman) is on the left, Mary
on the right; Elizabeth has placed her hand on Mary's stomach to
feel the baby. There is a gate and dovecote (with doves on the roof)
in the middle ground, and in the background a river, boats, and the
towers of a city.

In matutinis laud͛
Eus in adiutorium
meū intende · Domi
ne ad adiuuandum ꞏ

## Plate 9. The Annunciation to the Shepherds

*Introducing the Office of Prime (6 a.m.), the third of the Hours of the Virgin: it (like all those between Matins and Compline) commences with the words "Deus in adiutorium meum intende" (O God, come to my help).*

The shepherds keeping watch over their flock by night receive from an angel the announcement of the birth of Jesus in Bethlehem, and they hear a multitude of the heavenly host praising God. (The "host" is represented by four angels, with a scroll.) The shepherd on the right has stopped playing his bagpipe and is shading his face (in allusion to the light that shone round about them); the two on the left (the farther one a shepherdess) have fallen into attitudes of prayer. The sheep seem unconcerned, as does the sleeping sheepdog in the foreground. In the background across the winding stream are a meadow with a wheeled horse cart, more shepherds on the hill on the left, and (on the far right) a castle.

## Plate 10. The Nativity

*Introducing the Office of Terce (9 a.m.), the fourth of the Hours of the Virgin: it (like all those between Matins and Compline) commences with the words "Deus in adiutorium meum intende" (O God, come to my help).*

In the manger in Bethlehem where Jesus was born, Mary kneels in adoration before the tiny child, who lies naked on the ground; the ox and the ass (seen through the open door) are also kneeling. Joseph appears on the right with a lighted candle and a stick, two shepherds are observing the scene from the left, and a heavenly choir of angels appears above the thatched roof.

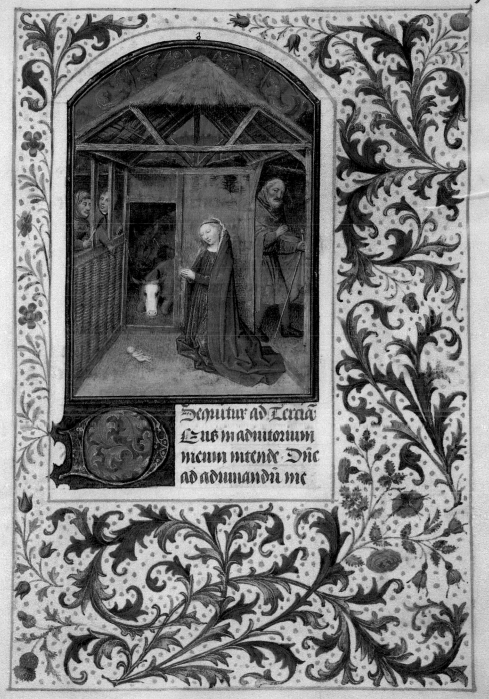

Sequitur ad Tertiā
Eus in adiutorium
meum intende. Dnc
ad adiuuandū me

## Plate 11. The Adoration of the Magi

*Introducing the Office of Sext (noon), the fifth of the Hours of the Virgin: it (like all those between Matins and Compline) commences with the words "Deus in adiutorium meum intende" (O God, come to my help).*

The Three Wise Men (Magi) have followed the star (visible above the thatched roof) to come and worship the newborn Jesus. Traditionally, they were represented as kings named Gaspar, Melchior, and Balthazar; they came from the east, the south, and the west; one was old, one young, and one in the prime of life; and they brought symbolic offerings of gold, frankincense, and myrrh. The old king has doffed his crown while kneeling before Jesus, and the other two are waiting their turns behind him; three servants stand in the left rear, and on the road beyond them is a troop of armed men. Mary holds the tiny Jesus so that the old king can kiss his foot, and Joseph at the far right has taken off his hat. The episode involving the Adoration of the Magi is celebrated in the Christian Year on January 6 as Epiphany, or the manifestation of Christ to the Gentiles.

Ad Sextam horam
Eus in adiutorium
meum intende Dne
ad adiuuandum me

## Plate 12. The Presentation in the Temple

*Introducing the Office of Nones (3 p.m.), the sixth of the Hours of the Virgin: it (like all those between Matins and Compline) commences with the words "Deus in adiutorium meum intende" (O God, come to my help).*

When Jesus was eight days old, Mary and Joseph brought him to the temple in Jerusalem, in accordance with Jewish law, to present him to the Lord. Mary, on the left, is presenting the infant Jesus at the altar. Joseph, behind her, is holding a basket of doves and a lighted candle, the traditional offering. The High Priest, kneeling on the right of the altar, wearing his ceremonial robes and gold pointed hat, is reaching out to receive Jesus. Nine other men and women (carefully distinguished by posture and expression, particularly eyes) are observing the presentation.

Ad nonam horam .
Eus in adiutorium
meum intende . Dñe
ad adiuuandum me

## Plate 13. The Flight into Egypt

*Introducing the Office of Vespers (6 p.m.), the seventh of the Hours of the Virgin: it (like all those between Matins and Compline) commences with the words "Deus in adiutorium meum intende" (O God, come to my help).*

Joseph, Mary, and Jesus flee into Egypt to avoid the slaying, ordered by Herod in order to kill Jesus, of all infants under the age of two. An angel warned Joseph in a dream to flee to Egypt, and the picture shows them on their journey. Joseph walks ahead, with a bundle on a stick over his shoulder and leading the donkey. Mary holds Jesus wrapped in her mantle and sits sidesaddle on the donkey. The road they have traveled curves into the far distance, where a group pursuing them on horseback can be seen beyond the river. Even further off a castle is built across the water, and a very large church-type building is on the left.

Ad vesperas horas ⸫
us in adiutorium
meum intende · Dne
ad adiuuandum me

## Plate 14. The Coronation of the Virgin

*Introducing the Office of Compline, or Completorium (9 p.m.), the eighth and last of the Hours of the Virgin: it commences with the words "Converte nos Deus salutaris noster" (Change our hearts, O God our salvation).*

Mary is seated, at the left, on an elaborate Gothic throne. A crown is already on her head, signifying that she is Queen of Heaven; her hands are together in prayer. The figure on the right represents God the Father, wearing a crown, with his right hand giving a blessing and his left hand holding an orb which symbolizes the world. In the rear, on either side of the throne, are ranks of angels.

Ad complectorium
Onuerte nos deus sa
salutaris noster Et
auerte iram tuam

## Plate 15. King David in Prayer

*Introducing the seven Penitential Psalms and Litany: the Office commences*
*with the beginning of Psalm 6, "Domine ne in furore tuo arguas me"*
*(O Lord, rebuke me not in thine anger).*

David, the supposed author of the psalms, has laid his harp against a
rock in the left foreground and is praying to God for forgiveness.
(The sin which was usually associated with his penitence was that
of having sent Uriah to certain death so that he might marry Uriah's
wife Bathsheba.) God is pictured in the sky, listening, wearing a
triple crown and holding an orb and cross, surrounded by angels.
Below, a white angel keeps watch. The landscape includes trees at
the left, water, and a fortified castle with drawbridge.

Les vij: psalmes de
penitance z psalm?
Omine ne in furore
tuo arguas me neq;

## Plate 16. The Virgin Enthroned

*Introducing two Prayers to the Holy Virgin: the first of the two prayers begins*
*"Obsecro te domina sancta maria" (I beseech thee, O Lady, Holy Mary).*

Mary is seated on a tall throne, ready to nurse her child Jesus. She is surrounded by six angels making music: the front one on the left is singing from a book, and the front two on the right are playing a lute and a harp.

Sensieut vne deuo
te orison de nredame
bsecro te domina :
sancta maria mat

## Plate 17. The Raising of Lazarus

*Introducing the Office of the Dead: it commences with the words "Placebo [domine in regione vivorum]" (I will please [thee, O Lord, in the land of the living]).*

Jesus has ordered Lazarus of Bethany to come forth, after having been four days in the grave. Lazarus is rising, with his grave clothes on, his hands lifted in prayer. The right hand of Jesus is raised in blessing Lazarus. Jesus is surrounded by the two sisters of Lazarus, Martha and Mary, and by four men; the faces of all of them reflect the miracle which has just been performed. This miracle is taken to represent the power over death and to prefigure the resurrection of Jesus and of all the dead before the last judgment.

Sen sic uwet bigilie?
des mors ap Slacebo ps
Jleri quoniam crau
diet dns noce ozonis